INTERGENERATIONAL TRAUMA

The Ghosts of Times Past

Table of Contents

Introduction

Many of the people that I have talked about intergenerational trauma typically start the conversation with the question, "What is intergenerational trauma?" It is not surprising that many people do not fully understand it, and many people tend to deny that it even exists. Society has had several different types of trauma brought to its attention over the last century that it was unaware of and did not believe previously existed. It is important to understand trauma and trauma-related disorders in order to fully grasp how intergenerational trauma affects individuals.

At the turn of the 20th century, the majority of society did not give credence to the effects of PTSD. In the 1940s, the first definitions of Post-Traumatic Stress Disorder were written down.

The first scientifically effective treatments were developed in the 1960s. In the 1980s and 1990s, the effects of combat-related PTSD were shown on television and in mainstream media as a result of the large numbers of Vietnam Veterans that were being affected by the disorder. Since then, research has also shed light on non-combat related PTSD such as domestic violence, refugees, sexual crimes, discrimination, and childhood trauma related types of PTSD. When one compares the length of time that trauma-related disorders have been studied compared to various other medical disorders, one realizes that we know relatively little about trauma compared to other conditions. The American Psychological Association defines trauma as "an emotional response to a terrible event like an accident, rape or natural disaster." One will often display shock immediately after the event and tend to even deny the event occurred. Exposure to trauma also leaves long-lasting effects such as unpredictable emotions, flashbacks, strained relationships and even physical symptoms like headaches or nausea.

There are several mental health diagnoses that occur as a re-sult of exposure to trauma. Post-Traumatic Stress Disorder (PTSD) receives the most media coverage among the psychological disor-ders that occur as a result of trauma. PTSD is commonly noted by the presence of four clusters of symptoms. Those symptoms in-clude re-experiencing the event, heightened arousal, avoidance, and negative thoughts and feelings. The DSM-V has divided PTSD into two subtypes to better categorize the particular symptomology experienced by the individual. The first subtype is the PTSD Preschool subtype. This type of PTSD addresses the developmental differences for children who are of preschool age. It is important to consider the presentation of young children's symptoms differently than those of adults due to the developmental differences between children and adults. The other subtype is the PTSD Dissociative subtype. This subtype is notable unique due to the individual's experiences of feeling detached from one's own mind or body. These individuals report feelings in which the world seems unreal, dreamlike, or distorted. In addition to PTSD, Acute Stress Disorder is commonly seen among individuals who have experienced trauma. Acute Stress Disorder (ASD) is different from PTSD in that symptoms last from to three days up to a month while PTSD requires symptoms to persist for more than one month.

Reactive Attachment Disorder (RAD) is commonly seen among individuals that have experienced trauma. RAD is seen in children with the disorder become evident before the age of five. Children with RAD are emotionally withdrawn from their caregivers. They fail to seek comfort when distressed and fail to respond to comforting. These children have experienced patterns of extremes in their care that are typically evidenced by neglect with regard to their most basic needs, repeated changes of primary caregivers that prevent the formation of attachments, and being raised in usual ways that limit the ability to for attachments for the child.

One should not that these symptoms are not be better account for by a diagnosis of autism spectrum disorder when a child is diagnosed with RAD.

The Center for Disease Controls have reported that individuals who suffer from PTSD and other trauma related disorders are at higher rates for the occurrence of various physical ailments such as cancers, ischemic heart disease, and chronic lung disease. Trauma in childhood has been found to correlate to lower levels of well-being in later life. Rates of suicide are significantly higher among individuals with trauma related disorders than the general public. Individuals that experience trauma related disorders have much higher levels of substance abuse, alcoholism, Tabaco use, and overall poorer well-being.

It is clear to see how trauma produce long lasting effects that impact the health and well-being of an individual. Looking at the numbers and statistics associated with trauma-related disorders and conditions, psychological and physical ailments can be clearly attributed to the impacts of the trauma or, at least, be contributed to the amplification of symptoms and adverse conditions. In treating and providing services to individuals that have experienced trauma, there are numerous barriers between the traumatized individual and achieving a better state of being. Intergenerational trauma typically plays a large part in creating these barriers and reinforcing them over through culture, learning, and repetition.

Intergenerational trauma is the carryover of the effects of trauma across generations. Intergenerational trauma has also been referred to as trans-generational trauma. When trauma is transmitted across multiple generations through repeated traumatic incidents, it leads to what many refer to as historical trauma or cultural trauma. This effect has taken different names depending on the field of study that examines it and attempts to explain the causes, correlations, and effects of the events. In essence, intergenerational trauma occurs when individuals experience the symptomology of trauma-related disorders due to the experiences of their parents and ancestors. This effect can be seen in several different cultures and groups of people as the traumas of the past can be seen to affect the individuals in the present even though those individuals never directly experienced the trauma.

Intergenerational trauma has been noted in the carryover effects of single trauma events that have happened to the parents such as has been seen in combat veterans and rape victims. These types of intergenerational trauma are referred to as single event transmissions. Single event transmissions have been shown to manifest in the children with symptoms comparable to those of the parent and as would be expected by an individual that had experienced trauma similar to the parent. In some cases, the transmission of trauma-related symptoms have skipped generations as seen in studies of holocaust survivors and their grandchildren.

Across multiple generations, the effects of intergenerational trauma have shown increases in the severity of symptoms if the trauma is perpetuated in a manner that is either real or imagined. Often, the effects of cultural norms will compound this impact as the individual's culture may devalue the negative feelings and effects of the intergenerational trauma. This devaluation of the individual may lead to continued re-traumatization resulting a persistent continuation of the transmission of trauma across many generations.

It is important to remember that there is a difference between cultural identity and historical trauma. It is very important for an individual to be able to connect with their culture and keep cultural values and ideas alive throughout his or her connections to the past. Historical trauma is the result of tragedies that have befallen a group of people resulting in maladaptive responses to later situations. Intergenerational trauma is escalated as the result of individuals perpetuating the trauma-related symptoms that came about as a result of historical trauma. The cultural history and identity should still be maintained and kept intact, but the Post-traumatic symptoms do not need to be carried on through the generations. This is a topic that has led to many debates regarding when a facet of a culture is a debilitating symptom created by historically trauma experiences that ancestors experienced and when it is just the way that an ethnic group of people are. Determining where to draw the line between culture and maladaptive practices often involves a critical examination of what is socially acceptable among differing ethical viewpoints.

Mass event transmissions occur as a part of an event or series of traumatic events that affect a large group of people. Examples of mass trauma events include the Holocaust, slavery, genocide, apartheid, and forced assimilation like the resettlement of Native Americans or Aboriginals in Australia. There are many different mass trauma events that have impacted cultures throughout history. Several mass trauma events have been studied in many different ways, but there are many events that have not adequately been studied and examined fully to understand the psychological and sociological impacts of all traumas.

In the case of long term mass event traumas, such as the resettlement of Native Americans, slavery in African-Americans, and the lost generation of the Aboriginals, the psychological issues and impacts of the ongoing trauma-related symptoms become associated with a part of that societal group's culture. For example, George was an African-American student that came from a typical middle class family. George did not experience any abuse growing up and did not have any negative experiences with law enforcement. George does, however, report that he feels anxious, "on edge", and hyper-vigilant around law enforcement officers. George claimed that he was afraid that the police will detain him and beat him. George's grandparents experienced oppression during the segregation of the 1950s and discrimination by police during the

1960s. George has never experienced the trauma that his grandparents did, but George is affected by their trauma and also the
trauma of his ancestors that suffered in slavery in the 1800s. There
are many cases of individuals like George that are of different
cultures, races, and ethnic groups that have exhibited symptoms of
anxiety and stress as the result of past trauma that had affected ancestors and family members.

When examining situations like this, there are many different
responses to why individuals experience these types of maladaptive responses to authority figures and various other situations that
result in individuals being affected by intergenerational trauma.
Throughout this book, we will attempt to explore some of the various theories on how trauma manifests in individuals across generations, how it is transmitted, and how one can attempt to free themselves from the bonds of the trauma that affected their ancestors.

What Happens During Trauma

When talking about trauma, it is important to understand what happens to an individual at a cognitive, neurological, and biological level as a result of trauma. The experience of trauma leads to changes in the individual just as anything that happens in the environment of an organism affects an organism. The things that we experience in life shape the way we see the world. Traumatic events have a heavy impact on the development of young individuals and also on the way that individuals perceive the world after their traumatic experience. This can be seen in the avoidance tendencies of soldiers who have returned from Iraq, Afghanistan, and Vietnam when exposed to large crowds. The traumatic experiences that these soldiers went through in combat created an aversion to areas with large numbers of people. Additionally, these same soldiers have reported feeling uncomfortable when they were not able to see where the exit to a building was or if they had their backs turned toward the exit. Prior to their deployment, these individuals did not have these types of concerns or fears that guided their behaviors. As a result of their experiences, their way of thinking had been changed to produce different perceptions of the world and the things that are threats to themselves.

Research has shown that traumatic events impact both brain development, memory, and cognitive functioning. The way this happens on a neurobiological level is by impacting the corticotrophin-releasing factor (CRF)/hypothalamic-pituitary-adrenal (HPA) axis system. This system serves to balance the body's reaction to stress through the release and regulation of norepinephrine and cortisol. Hypothalamus releases CRF into the body, with stimulation of adrenocorticotropic hormone (ACTH) release from the pituitary, resulting in glucocorticoid and cortisol being released from the adrenal glands. This release of glucocorticoid and cortisol creates a negative feedback effect on the axis at the level of the pitui-

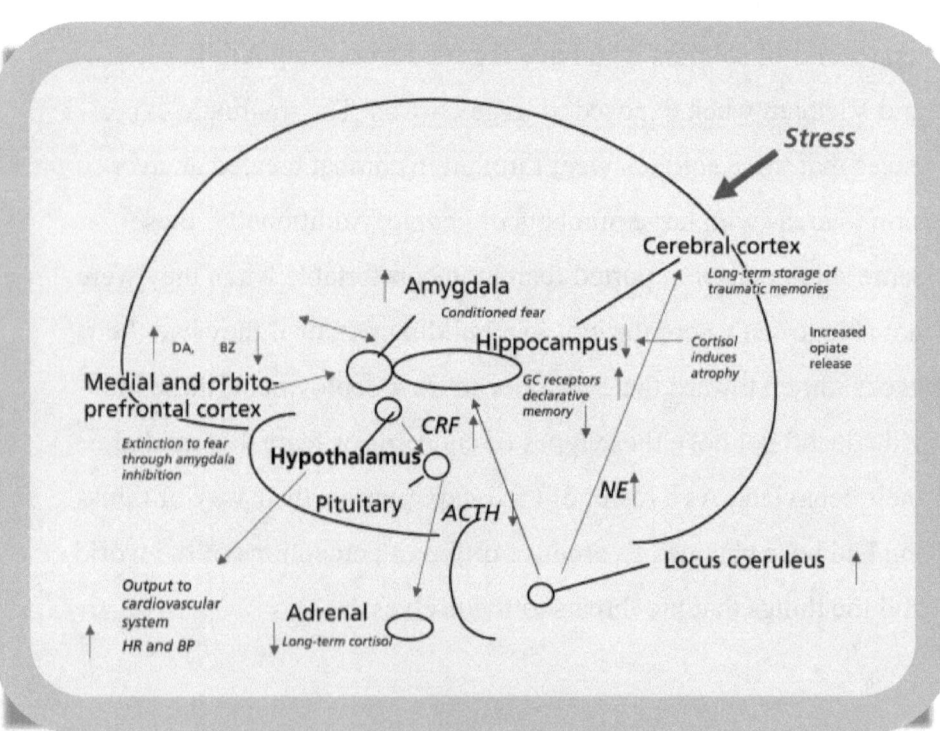

tary gland and central brain sites including hypothalamus and hippocampus. Cortisol generates a survival response in humans that is often referred to as a flight or fight response. Additionally, it stimulates various neural centers in the brain responsible for increasing alertness and vigilance behaviors.

These functions are essential for coping with threats and performing critical tasks during periods of elevated levels of risk of harm. In individuals with trauma-related dysfunction, this process basically gets stuck in an active state or state that easily reactivated. As a result of prolonged, repeated, or chronic exposure traumatic events, one may develop a dependency or tolerance to the neurochemical transmitters released into the bodies system as a result of trauma. What this means in simpler terms is that the body becomes used to the state of heightened arousal that occurs during traumatic experiences. The individual often begins to desire the rush of adrenaline that occurs as a result of the "flight or fight" response. The body becomes dependent on the rush of neurotransmitters and hormones that serve as the body's response to stabilize. When the individual is in a normal or non-response state, they feel as though something is missing or not quite right. This type of dependency often results in individuals taking part in adrenaline-inducing behaviors. They are often seen as "Adrenaline Junkies." In some cases, individuals find safe outlets to achieve this state of elevated levels of stress responses. In cases where safe and controlled outlets are not available to the individual, more dangerous behaviors often occur such as reckless driving, substance abuse, domestic violence, and various illegal and hazardous behaviors.

Cognitive theories of psychology provide a useful insight into the mental process of individuals who have experienced trauma. When working with individuals that have been exposed to trauma or suffer from trauma-related disorders, it is important to be aware of the differences in processing information for these individuals. The differences in learning, comprehending, and responding are not only useful for psychologists and therapists to be aware. Understanding these differences are essentially useful for social workers, teachers, parents, caregivers, friends, and family. When one takes these differences into consideration, frustrations, arguments, and emotional-fatigue can be greatly reduced as one can modify and adjust his or her approach to working with individuals who suffer from trauma-related disorders.

To understand this perspective, one should be familiar with a few psychological concepts. The first thing to understand is the

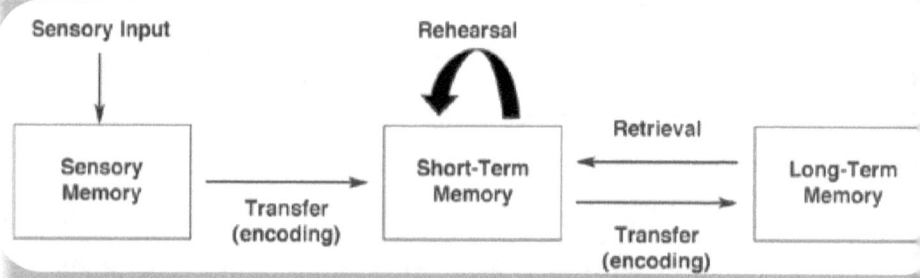

working memory model. The working model of memory contains

three parts: sensory memory, short-term memory (also called working memory), and long-term memory. This model serves as a way of understand how information is processed in the mind. These concepts do not serves physical elements that exist in the brain but as abstract concepts for how information is stored, processed, and retrieved. Sensory memory, often referred to as the sensory register, allows environmental information to be retained for a short to be processed. The sensory memory typically only holds information for a fraction of a second as it makes its way into our consciousness. The information is then transferred from the sensory to the short-term memory through the use of attention. The short-term memory attends to items and concepts to make use of them. The short-term memory is often referred to as the working memory because it does all the active and effortful work with ideas and concepts in the mind. As the working memory attends to items, it retrieves information from the sensory memory in order to understand information. The working memory can usually manipulate five to nine items at a time. Items are only stored in the short term memory for ten to fifteen seconds before it is lost unless the information is given attention by the individual.

The working memory attends to concepts and items in short-term memory through processes of rehearsal to encode the items into long-term memory. Typically, this process of rehearsal is accomplish by rote repetition or by elaboration of the information. Long-term memory can hold items in a permanent manner and can hold a large or almost unlimited number of items. Long term memory can be thought of as the place where all memories are stored until they are needed. When the memories are needed, the working memory retrieves the items from the long term memory. Items are easier to retrieve when they have been better encoded into long-term memory by making more connections to other concepts and ideas. After retrieving an item back from long-term memory, the working memory can then manipulate the item to be used with other information for application and learning of complex thought, critical thinking, and knowledge development.

By this point, one may wonder what all this has to do with trauma related disorders. It has everything to do with trauma-related disorders. In 1992, Dr. Michael Eysenck and Dr. Manuel Calvo explained how research showed that anxiety impaired the effectiveness of working memory on attending to pieces of information for storage and retrieval from long-term memory. Working memory completes tasks through the utilization of attention. In the case of individuals with trauma-related disorders such as PTSD, the working memory is continuously preoccupied with the effects of the experienced trauma. The trauma is continually revisited by individuals and creates anxiety. The re-experiencing of negative thoughts, emotions, and feelings that were the result of experienced trauma causes the individuals to be on edge, and the individual devotes cognitive energy or attention to preparing for repeated trauma. This can be explained by the hyper vigilance symptoms and pervasiveness of the post-traumatic stress.

Due to the working memory's preoccupation with the trauma and potential for new trauma, the individual only uses a limited amount of attention with regards to task such as learning, remembering, and acquiring new skills. This can be seen as a contributory factor to why a disproportionate number of children who have experienced trauma also have difficulties in school. In addition to difficulties learning, individuals also experience diminished abilities to retrieve information from long-term memory. As the individual is continually devoting cognitive resources to addressing the anxiety caused by the trauma, mental fatigue sets in for the individual.

There are numerous ways in which one can explain how trauma affects brain development, cognitive functioning, and various mental processes. The end result for all of these various theories, studies, and models is that trauma has an adverse impact on the long-term well-being of an individual when left untreated. These impacts can be mitigated by treatment and may vary depending upon the resiliency of the individual. However, the impacts of trauma are still present and have both short-term and long-term effects upon the individual.

The Holocaust

Numerous research articles have explored how the children of holocaust survivors presented PTSD-like symptoms even though they had never experienced trauma. In the research, the children were found to be hyper-vigilant and untrusting of others. The children also reported that they felt different from their peers and realized that they acted differently also. The research did address that the populations that were looked at were clinical populations that had come to the attention of mental health professionals by self-referral. Additionally, due to the nature of the holocaust,

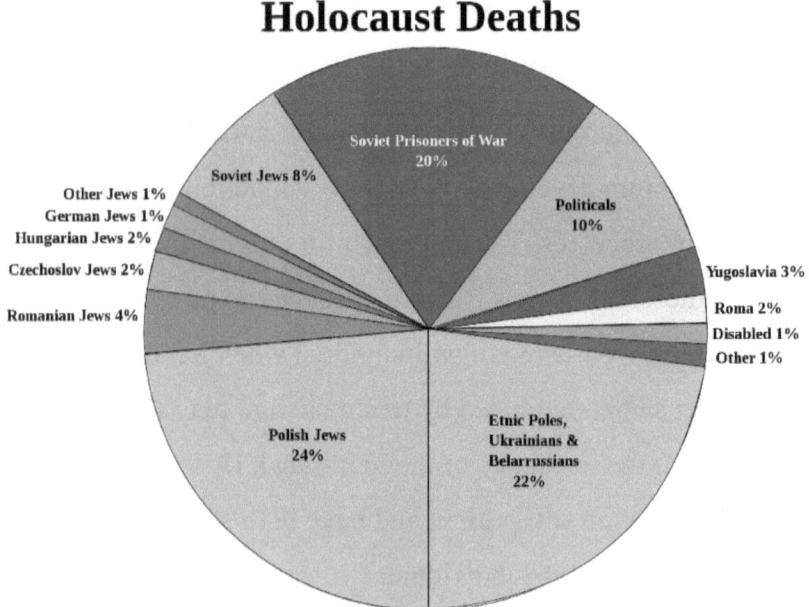

Holocaust Deaths

random sampling would be impossibility preventing a true experiment.

Studies have been completed to address a variety of theories that has been used to explain the appearance of the symptoms in subsequent generations. The secondary PTSD could be explained as a symptom of deep understanding of the following generation about the prior generation in an attempt to understand their parents' struggles during the World War II era. The symptoms were also explored as being the product of storytelling compounded by silent periods. An evolutionary approach to the behaviors poses that the symptoms serve to be the younger generations' reactions to the parents' attempts at teaching their children how to survive in times of persecution. This could be seen as an explanation based the concept of individuals' attempting to aid their genes in being based on through time. To promote the chances of lineage continuation, the survivors of the older generation develop attachment-styles and behave in ways that aide their children's survival based on the experiences of their lives when they were younger.

Dr. Baranowsky, founder and director of Traumatology Institute in Toronto, Canada, proposed that the transmission of trauma between generations could serve to set the expectations of clinicians treating PTSD sufferers. In light of such research, one should also look for symptoms of intergenerational transmission in the children of clients suffering from PTSD. The research does not provide a likelihood of transmission due to the claimed impossibility of designing such an experiment.

Dr. Dani Rowland-Klein and Rosemary Dunlop performed groundbreaking research on the effect of trauma on the descendants of Holocaust survivors. They interviewed six individuals who were children of Holocaust survivors to determine what themes were present across the individuals that would have contributed to transmission of trauma across generations. The research revealed a number of themes that were consistent across the sample. First, the sample displayed a number of themes revolving around their parents' style of parenting. These themes were more pronounced and notable in the comparison of their parents to other parents. Additionally, concerns about overprotection and issues with separation were commonly seen as themes in parenting. The children also heavily identified with their parent's experiences in a subjective understanding of what the concentration camp experience was like for their parents. An additional finding in the study was that the second generation had showed a heightened state of awareness about the parents' status as being Holocaust survivors through both overt and covert understandings of their parents' story of survival. As a result of these factors, a message of mistrust and fear were transmitted to the second generation through messages about a need to survive in dangerous situations.

The researchers utilized an interview format to conduct the

study with the small sample size that consisted of only females, which was a weakness of the study. Despite the weaknesses of the study, it did present a detailed look at the individual cases and the emerging themes that appeared across the individuals. The sample was a non-clinical sample, which serves to be unique because the individuals reported several pathological symptoms associated with PTSD such as hyper-vigilance, mistrust, nightmares, and persistent fears. Researchers also served to divide the methods of transmission into two categories that include conscious and unconscious transmissions of trauma. In making this distinction between the methods of transmission, the study presented the behaviors of the parents as being a dynamic interaction between the types of forces that magnifies the effect of transmission of trauma across generations.

With a wide array of research regarding Holocaust survivors and their children, studies have also been conducted regarding the grandchildren of holocaust. Throughout these studies, several themes have emerged regarding the effects of the transmission. Typically, the transmission is typically viewed as being either an impact of nature or nurture. When viewing the transmission through the lens of nature or biological transmission, the field of study is referred to as epigenetics. When one first hears this notion, one may say that this sounds like genes trying to explain everything. It is a little more complex than that. The genetic code does not simply change as a result of survival of the fittest or the weeding out of undesirable survival traits as seen in traditional evolutionary theory.

Holocaust survivors experienced in extreme trauma in concentration camps and the ghettos of Europe. In response to this stress, the body produces certain neurotransmitters and hormones to aid in survival. These chemical messengers are essential for survival and stress reduction. A notable effect is the reduced levels of cortisol in the children of Holocaust survivors. Most people are aware that high levels of cortisol have impacts an individual's health by tearing down muscle tissue, slowing down healing processes, and impacting cell regeneration. However, cortisol is essential to survival. You cannot live without cortisol. One might expect to find high levels of cortisol in the Holocaust survivors and their children. To the contrary, it is the opposite. Children and grandchildren of Holocaust survivors have actually shown drastically lower than normal levels of cortisol. When cortisol levels are low, the individual is at a higher risk for anxiety disorders and will have difficulty coping with stress. This phenomena predisposes the children of Holocaust survivors to not only Generalized Anxiety Disorder but also sets the stage for PTSD-like symptoms that are indicative of intergenerational trauma.

Epigenetic research explains that these low cortisol levels in the children and grandchildren can be explained by the experiences and the survival reactions of individuals during the Holocaust. In the concentration camps, it was fear clear that the inmates were starved. From the photographs, videos, and evidence, this is very clear. The survivors looked like "walking skeletons." Of the atrocities committed, the starvation of individuals is often the first thing that one notices. In order to stay alive in such extremes, the human body goes into survival mode. As a response to starvation, the body produces reduces enzyme activity. This reduction keeps higher levels of free cortisol in the body and maximizes the amount of metabolic fuels such as glucose in the kidneys and liver. Once the individual is no longer in survival state, the body releases high levels of enzymes to break up the cortisol in the body. In the case of severe trauma, the amount of enzymes released is substantially high.

When the Holocaust survivor is then pregnant, the mother has lower levels of cortisol but is then producing high amounts of the reducing enzymes. The fetus often produces additional reducing enzymes to protect the fetus from the cortisol that is present in the mother's system. In epigenetics, this process helps prepare the child for an environment that is similar to that of the parents. In the case of Holocaust survivors, this results in the child producing much higher rates of the reducing enzymes to prepare for a high-stress environment outside of the womb. Once the child is born and develops, it continues to produce the reducing enzymes at higher levels than other children. Therefore, the child is prepared to compensate for the stress effects that one would experience in a concentration camp, but the levels of stress and need for survival are not as high as the body expects. Cortisol is not stored in as high levels as would be needed in such a survival state. As a result, the child produces cortisol at a regular rate with that is then counteracted by the cortisol-reducing enzymes during development. Throughout development, the child begins to produce less cortisol as the body adjusts to less stress; however, the body does not reduce the production of the enzymes used to break up cortisol. Upon maturing, the child is found to have very high levels of the enzymes used to break up cortisol and very low levels of cortisol. As a result of these hormone levels, the individual's body is less equipped to handle stress. They are at a higher risk for age-related metabolic syndromes, including obesity, hypertension, and insulin resistance. Additionally, they are more vulnerable to the effects of stress and trauma and more likely to experience PTSD-like symptoms.

In examining the intergenerational of Holocaust survivors through lens of the nurture point of view, one explains the transmission of symptoms by way of learning theories and theories of childhood development. When looking at the transmission through this lens, one should remember that people do what they know or more specifically people do what they have learned. If someone has learned to do something, that person will do what they have learned. Human beings are creatures of habit, and things are learned habitually and through repeated exposure.

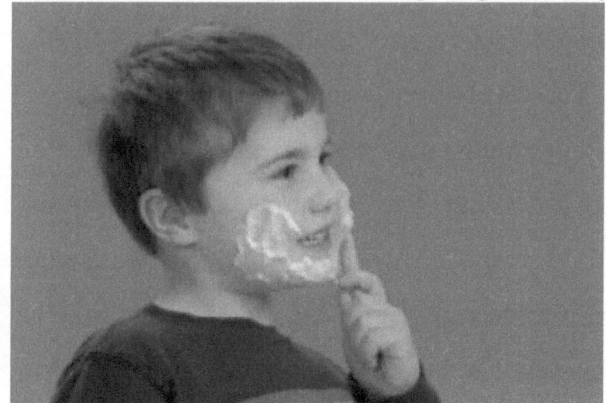

Observational learning is a common concept that has visited and studied throughout the theories of child development and how individuals learn. Observational learning is where an individual learns how to do something or how the world works by observing actions or their environment. In a child's environment, they learn most directly from their parents or caregivers. For example, young child watches his father shaving. He watches the technique and methods used. He watches how the father applies shaving cream. He observes the motions of how the razor is drawn across the face. He watches how the father then cleans off his face. The child takes in how this process works and all the minor details. The child may do this once or multiple times. The process is then stored in the child's memory and is re-examined in detail several times. This is how the child learns this process by observation only. Later in life, the child will know how to shave or at least the general procedure.

Similarly, the child learns how to cope with stressors by observation. Observation learning is often associated in this fashion with cycles of violence, cycles of addition, and many other behaviors that are consistent across generations. In the case of intergenerational trauma, it is a cycle of trauma or least a cycle of the effects of trauma. The child observes how the parents cope with trauma. The child or parents may not even consciously be aware of what they are observing. The child may watch the parent display signs of paranoid around crowds. The child may watch the parent become uncomfortable and avoid triggers. The child may observe biases and stigmas. The behavior observed may be as clear as direct and clear prejudice or it may be very subtle. This behavior becomes magnified in the child's mind as a coping skill or indicator of danger as in the case of the child observing the parent's avoidance of triggers. As the child observes, he learns these behaviors and then mimics the behaviors. Parent and child are often not consciously aware of the behaviors and biases that are developed. In many cases, the parent does not intend to develop a bias in the child, but it does happen through learning.

As the child grows into an adult, these learned behaviors continue to be present without intervention. Sometimes the learned behaviors can become magnified. For example, the parent may avoid furnaces and fireplaces as they may serve as a trigger for the trauma that was experienced during the Holocaust. The parent may have shown panic or an unintentional reaction while the child was observing caused by the trigger of a fireplace. The child, then, develops the notion that fireplaces are incredibly dangerous. They should be avoided. They child may associate the fireplace without the reaction of the parent. The child may develop exaggerated startle responses to seeing fire. This is an example, but one can see how the effect can be magnified and often is magnified by the child.

Some of the effects of observational learning are mitigated by social interactions such as school-aged learning and exposure to individuals outside the family that challenge irrational beliefs. In many cases, these irrational beliefs and fears that have been deeply ingrained into the child's unconscious belief system. As a result, single exposure to challenges does not adequately unseat the maladaptive belief that was developed by the child through observational learning. Humans are stubborn creatures, and it is difficult to unlearn what has been learned by repeated exposure. In many instances, the children have observed the trauma-related symptoms by repeated exposure to situations in which the parent has reacted in maladaptive manner or as a result of their post-traumatic symptoms. Repeated observations make it harder for the child to challenge beliefs and the responses even if the individual is making a conscious effort. The maladaptive response and belief becomes almost reflexive.

In the case of intergenerational trauma of Holocaust survivors, it is useful to look at the transmission in the light of a dynamic between nature and nurture. It is not typically transmitted solely by one means. The transmission typically occurs as a combination of the two explanations of the transmission interacting with one another. In examining the dynamic approach to intergenerational trauma, the nature theory lays the groundwork for predisposition. An individual is at a higher risk of developing trauma related symptoms due to their genetic or chemical make-up. When remembering the epigenetic theory, one should note that this sets the stage for symptoms, but it alone does not determine that an individual will display symptoms of PTSD as a result of the trauma experienced by the prior generation. The nurture part builds up on the framework for trauma that has been laid by the epigenetic view. The child observes the symptomology of the parents and learns behaviors. They learn to avoid the triggers of the adult. They learn responses to triggers. They view crowds as dangerous. The child sets up a belief system of fear and anxiety that is similar to that of the parents. This creates an optimal environment for the younger generation to develop maladaptive responses to triggers and experience stress reactions as a result.

Native American Trauma

When taking into account the effects of intergenerational trauma, Native Americans are at the forefront of the groups examined. There have been numerous studies conducted to understand how the trauma occurred and how it is passed from generation to generation. When trying to understand fully the impacts of trauma, one should be aware of what the trauma event or events were that occurred first. After being aware of the events, one should determine what beliefs are created as a result of the traumatic events and then how they result in consequential actions that affect the present generation. This format is often referred to as the ABCs of trauma. A is the activating event (traumatic event). B is the belief that is formed as a result. C is the consequence of the irrational or disturbing beliefs. This ABC formula is commonly seen in Cognitive Behavioral Therapy (CBT) Models and Rational Emotive Behavioral Therapy (REBT) models to explain the development of anxiety and fears. The ABC is useful in helping individuals to understand the mechanisms behind PTSD and

trauma-related disorders as the disorders are based in anxiety that is created as a result of the experienced trauma.

In the case of the intergenerational trauma of Native Americans, the trauma can be looked at as six unresolved traumas that have cumulated into highly concentrated historical trauma that is commonly seen across many Native American tribes. Initially, there was the first contact with Europeans. During this time, native people were introduced to new diseases and addictive substances such as alcohol. This time period serves as the traumatic shock of the first contact.

The next period of trauma was economic competition phase. During this time, Native Americans were persecuted for their religious beliefs and were exposed to manipulation when they attempted to trust Europeans. Third phase is often referred to as the extermination period. During this phase, many Europeans were seen as wanting to exterminate Native Americans. This led to many Native Americans experiencing something similar to

genocide as their people were being massacred in large numbers. This also led to many individuals experiencing symptoms similar to refugees in crisis.

The subjugation phase was the fourth period of trauma that Native Americans experienced. During this phase, many Native Americans were relocated and confined to reservations. After the experience of trauma that was caused by the Europeans, the Native Americans were then forced to be dependent on the individuals who had oppressed them. This was the result of the Native Americans having their lands taken from them during the previous periods. During this phase of history, it was common for many Native peoples to explain their state of being as a sense of hopelessness and felt as if they had no way of maintaining their security. This is an important thing to note as security is listed as a basic human need according to theories such as Maslow's Hierarchy of needs, and hopelessness is straightforward way of describing depression.

The fifth phase of trauma was the boarding school period. During this time, children were removed from families and placed in boarding schools that were intended to assimilate the children into US culture. This movement had terrible results on the families that were subjected to it. Many children experienced severe beatings and abuse in the boarding schools. Young girls were raped by the caregivers in the schools. Many children were malnourished. Additionally, the family unit was destroyed as a resulted. In society, the family unit is substantial to the culture. The family unit provides for the most basic form of societal norms for people. It serves as a microcosm of how a society is to function. Through the observation of the parents, children learn how to be parents themselves when they are older. As a result of these boarding schools, there was a generation of Native Americans who were confused about their identity, many customs and languages were lost or destroyed, and countless numbers of children were emotional, physically, and sexually abused throughout a large part

of their childhood.

The sixth phase of trauma has been referred to as the termination period. During this time frame, many Native Americans were relocated to urban areas. Many were oppressed due to their religious views. Racism was common place during this era. The racism experienced by Native Americans during this time frame was much like that experienced by African-Americans during the de-segregation era. Native Americans were often treated like second-class citizens. During this time, the Native Americans continued to lose their native languages, culture, customs, and sense of self. They were left feeling like a people lost to the changes of time.

As a result of the numerous traumatic experiences of Native Americans, a culture of grief has developed over several generations. When examining research across various Native American populations, trends of internalized feelings of oppression, depression, anger, and frustration appear to be common themes. Individuals have been commented that they had been told throughout their lives that they were dumb or substandard humans.

Lisa Grayshield, a professor of counseling and educational psychology at New Mexico State University, recently conducted research on the perspectives of Native American elders on the historical trauma of their people and its effects. During the research, Dr. Grayshield and her team interviewed tribal leaders from six different tribes. The elders explained how they remembered being humiliated and belittled due to their race when they were younger. Several individuals made connections between the current internalized oppression and the imposed values systems that were forced upon them during the boarding schools of the earlier twentieth century.

As the individuals of prior generations experienced trauma, they developed maladaptive coping skills to deal with the impacts of PTSD. These maladaptive skills have developed over several generations with each generation adding new skills to those learned from the previous generations. For example, the generations that experienced trauma as a result of being force-relocated to reservations developed the initial symptoms of PTSD such as hyper-vigilance and night terrors. Their young children initially observe the parent's coping with these symptoms by being paranoid, being dependent on alcohol, and various other strategies.

The younger generation is, then, exposed to new trauma by being placed in boarding schools and all the terrible experiences that came with the boarding schools. These children then grew up to develop new skills cope with their own traumatic experiences. This second generation combines the coping skills that they observed as children from their parents with their newly developed maladaptive strategies to cope with their trauma. The compounding of trauma upon trauma is commonly seen in cases of intergenerational trauma. In the case of Native Americans' intergenerational, the trauma is much more chronic than most examples of intergenerational trauma. In addition to the trauma being compounded by its reoccurrence over several generations, the trauma is also amplified by the creation of a disconnect between generations due to the remove of children from their homes by the individuals that are viewed as the ones that have been oppressing and persecuting their families for many generations.

This three-pronged trauma impact on the second generation produces much more pronounced symptoms than typical PTSD. Some people have presented the argument that individuals who have come from families with a history of PTSD tend to be more resilient in overcome trauma. The logic to the argument is that the parents served as models of how to cope with trauma. As a result, the children have a basis from which to develop skills in handling the effects of trauma in more productive manner. Unfortunately, this is not true of most cases. The parents do serve as models of how to handle trauma, but historically, PTSD symptoms have been greatly misunderstood and stigmatized. Native American populations have had fewer resources to mental health care due in part to being discriminated against by European populations and due in part to the destruction of their traditional culture and resources by the various cultural traumas that they have experienced throughout history. Therefore, the coping skills of the parent generation are often maladaptive due to a lack of resources available to develop effective and healthy coping skills. In the absence of treatment, the parent generation have often self-medicated through the use of alcohol and drug abuse. This self-medication is often seen as one of the contributing factors to higher rates of alcoholism among Native American populations. The younger generations, therefore, do not have effective role models for the development of healthy coping strategies but have models that are maladaptive and often strongly displaying the symptoms of individuals suffering from severe traumatic experiences.

When comparing different Native American families, the presence of intergenerational trauma effects are less pronounced among families that have been able to retain their cultural heritage. This particular effect is seen as the result of individuals being able to develop a higher level of resilience as a result of being able to maintain their cultural norms in the face of great adversity over many generations. Over generations, these families have been able to achieve a higher state of well-being on average as compared to families that have lost their cultural connections due to the boarding schools and assimilation efforts of the early twentieth century.

The impact of trauma upon Native Americans has clearly been accumulative effect as opposed to a single event. Many of the methods that were present in Holocaust survivors are also present in the case of Native Americans. The genetic influence of epigenetic predispositions is commonly seen as present in Native Americans along with the transmission of trauma-related behaviors through observational learning. In the case of Native Americans, the effect of intergenerational trauma is much more pronounced as the trauma has been across multiple generations. In addition, the beliefs are often more conscious than unconscious. The younger generations are more aware and more accepting of the biases against Europeans or white people than the Holocaust survivors are aware of individuals of German descent.

Several factors lead to the differences between Holocaust survivors and Native Americans with regard to the impacts of intergenerational trauma. In the case of Holocaust survivors, the atrocities of the concentration camps were made clear. There was never attempt by the media to downplay how terrible the war crimes were. During the Nuremburg Trials, the perpetrators of the crimes against humanity were brought to justice and were sentenced for their inhuman treatment of millions of people. For the Native American people, there was no trial for the perpetrators of the crimes committed against them. There was no justice. Many of the organizations that Native Americans see as responsible for their suffering were never held accountable for the atrocities that were committed. Due to the lack of justice, the sense of loss is compounded for the survivors. This leads to a sense of hopelessness and helplessness. In addition to the PTSD-like symptoms, the younger generations are at a higher risk for depression.

Native Americans also differ from the Holocaust survivors due to the loss of their culture and the destruction of the family unit in the case of Native Americans. Jewish individuals typically have strong family ties and bonds to their heritage. After World War II, the state of Israel was founded in 1947 which served to mitigate some of the effects of the Holocaust had upon individuals of Jewish heritage. This strengthened the bonds of many Holocaust survivors to their heritage and strengthened the family unit. As a result of strong family units, substance abuse, alcohol abuse, and crime rates among Jewish populations has traditionally been lower than those of non-Jewish populations. The family connections served as a buffer to some of the pronounced effects of PTSD symptoms such as self-treatment of symptoms through substance abuse.

In the case of Native Americans, the family unit was severely impacted by the assimilation efforts that occurred during the board school era. As a result, the family ties and connections to one's heritage were severed. Instead of creating higher levels of ethical behavior, the board schools did the opposite. As a result, substance abuse, alcohol abuse, and crime rates have been disproportionately higher among Native American populations. As a result of the separation of younger generations from the cultural ties, many individuals have reduced resilience in addition to a predisposition to anxiety-related symptoms. When the younger generations become adults, they are left with minimal coping skills to deal with psychological stressors. In order to manage the stress and the body's reaction to stress, many individuals will then self-treat through substance abuse and alcohol abuse due to a lack of resources available to them.

When the younger generation has children, their children will then learn maladaptive coping skills for stress from the parents and will also be genetically more vulnerable to trauma-related symptoms much like the children of Holocaust survivors. In Native Americans, the impacts of intergenerational trauma create a vicious cycle and become imbedded into the culture of the Native American people. This process leads to very pronounced prejudice towards individuals that are outside of their cultural group along with an avoidance to seeking treatment.

In the case of Native Americans, it is easy to see why they would avoid outsiders and treatment when taking into consideration how history is passed along in their culture. Native Americans have traditionally passed their history along in narrative form. Many cultures do this, but it is highly pronounced in Native American culture. Basically, the older generation will tell stories of how things were when they were young to the younger generations. The stories will be passed along from one generation to the next by storytelling. This form of relaying tales across generations has been essential to the development of civilizations, agriculture, science, and people's general way of life. It is how younger generations learn how to explicitly do things and explicitly learn about the world they may not have been able to observe. It is a way to learn about danger without being exposed to it and to learn about things that benefit them without having to commit trial and error work experiencing losses along the way.

Storytelling also plays a part in the transmission of intergenerational trauma. Researchers have found that silence about the trauma between family members and nostalgia contributed to the effects of the trauma. Nostalgia served to define to the younger generations how life was so drastically changed by the traumatic events of the past. Grandparents tell stories to grandchildren about how much better life was before the traumatic event and reflect that things were never the same after. Since all the children know is what life is like after the trauma, they assume a role of individuals that were directly affected by the traumatic events even though they never personally experienced the events.

Through interviews, researchers have noted that younger generations responded to the older generations when discussing the trauma as if they experienced the events themselves also. The best example was given when one of the children of a survivor answered questions about the survivor asked about events that occurred during the trauma, which happened before the younger individual was born. The traumatic events were discussed among family members rarely. The scarcity of the stories of trauma enriches the stories with a sense of novelty. The elders mentioned the stories only a few times to the younger generation so that the silence between the times that it is discussed strengthens the traumatic events and provides a connection for the younger generation to the events. The younger generation is often referred to as a "hinge" generation that is not yet free from the effects of the trauma but still a step toward making the trauma a notable history of their culture. In the case of Native Americans, there have been several "hinge" generations that have attempted to mitigate the long standing effects of trauma from prior generations.

This research serves to show how storytelling between generations serves to provide a tie between the recent generations and the current generation so that the scars of a specific trauma carry on through history. This shows how that intergenerational transmission serves to display how severe a traumatic occurrence is based upon how relevant the experience feels for proceeding generations. The effect of the trauma can be seen also by the way that younger generations also see the trauma as separating them from the nostalgia of the past that is magnified by silence.

By looking at the impacts that intergenerational trauma has had on Native Americans, one can note the impacts have been long standing and deeply impacted the entire culture of the people. In more recent generations, attempts have been made to mitigate the impacts of the numerous events that have impacted many prior generations. Even though positive steps have been made in the direction of change through new policies and concessions to make up for the impacts of historically significant trauma, there is still a long ways to go in addressing the issues that have built up over time.

Treatment and Change

The treatment of trauma-related disorders has a long history, but the evidence-based treatment of these disorders is a relatively new thing. Post-Traumatic Stress Disorder (PTSD) is nowadays the most commonly and widely known disorder related to trauma. PTSD, however, was not recognized as a diagnosable disorder until 1980 in adults and was not recognized in children until 1987. The treatment of PTSD has had a long and dark history. Over the years, the stigmas and misconceptions have waned over time to give way to more effective treatments, but many of the historical treatments of trauma related disorders tended to cause additional trauma that has led many individuals to be cautious of seeking help. The effects of historical treatments for trauma-related disorders in creating barriers to treatment is often seen as having similarities to how Intergenerational Trauma occurs.

One of the earliest noted treatments for trauma was around 2000 BC when tribes in modern-day Russia ingested poisonous mushrooms to counteract symptoms similar to PTSD-like symptoms. The mushrooms produced a euphoric state with delusions, which replace the fear and dread that is normally experienced during PTSD-related flashbacks. The ancient Greeks told trauma victims to get married to help with their PTSD and anxiety-related symptoms. The Vikings drank deer urine to help cope with symptoms. During the middle ages, Europeans attempt to purge the body of PTSD symptoms by taking laxatives. The Inca of South America were found to chew on Coca leaves to overcome their combat-related anxiety.

During the nineteenth century, a few treatments began to emerge that resembled modern treatments for PTSD and trauma-related disorders. In Japan, Dr. Genyu Imaizumi developed an approach to treating anxiety called persuasion therapy during the 1850s. The approach was fundamentally similar to modern Cognitive Behavior Therapy (CBT) and Rational Emotive Behavioral Therapy (REBT). Rest Therapy was an approach developed during the American Civil War that consisted of bed rest, a milk diet, massage, and electrical shock. Rest therapy, therefore, served as one of the earliest treatment to utilize electricity for the treatment of anxiety. Psychiatric medications, such as Potassium Bromide, were developed to treat individuals suffering from trauma-related disorders and anxiety disorders. Potassium Bromide was the forerunner of Barbital and Phenobarbital. During the late nineteenth century, early forms of psychotherapy emerged in Europe as treatments for PTSD symptoms.

During the early to mid-twentieth century, a variety of treatments for PTSD emerged that could be seen as highly questionable today. The questionable approaches can be seen as stemming from the denial of PTSD as a legitimate condition during those time periods. During World War I, common practices included the use of tranquilizers, placebos, and the surgical implantation of metal balls in the larynx of soldiers. The tranquilizers were used by the Russians and served to make the soldiers functional enough to return to the front lines with little to no resolution to the soldier's symptoms. The placebos were used to make the soldiers think that they were getting treatment when they were not receiving any

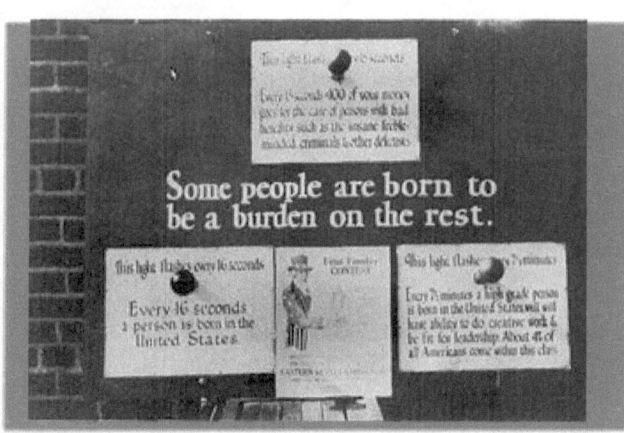

treatment. The metal balls placed in the larynx did nothing more than allow the soldiers to make sounds when they attempted to scream in terror

from flashbacks.

During World War II, the stigma of PTSD being experienced only by weak individuals was still present, but the increasing psychological causalities brought attention to the condition as being something more than a symptom of being weak. During the war, several clinicians attempted to treat anxiety using a variety of approaches. Captain Joseph Campbell, a military doctor, treated

patients with an approach including rest, work, and a form of brief psychoanalysis. Meanwhile, others used a mixture of hypnosis, drugs, and cathartic reliving of traumatic experiences.

During the 1950s, several psychotherapeutic interventions were develop to advance the treatment of trauma-related disorders. One of the most notable treatments was Systematic Desensitization. This therapeutic approach is based off of research in the study of learning and behavioral theory. What that basically means is that the approach is based off research in how people learn and how their behavior is driven by learning new things to replace old things. It is fairly simple practice and is at the basis for many PTSD treatments today. Systematic Desensitization allows one to rewire the brain by learning new things.

This treatment consists of three steps. First, one must identify the item that causes the anxiety. In the case of trauma-related disorders, the items that cause anxiety is referred to as triggers. Individuals who suffer from these disorders typically have multiple triggers. It is important to rank the triggers from least stressful to most stressful when identifying the triggers. The ranking of triggers will serve to help in determining the best approach for treatment in the later steps. Next, the individual learns techniques that are called coping strategies. These coping strategies are incompatible responses to the stress reactions. Examples of coping strategies include deep breathing, muscle relaxation, and various techniques that are typically producing a calming effect. In the final step, the anxiety producing item is then coupled with the coping technique. When coupling the anxiety producing items with the coping technique, it is best to start with the least stressful item and gradually work one's way up to more stressful items. The process allows the individual to become more aware of how their body is responding to triggers. Overtime, the individual will have less and less pronounced reactions to the triggers until the symptoms are barely noticed. It is important to note that not always will the negative responses to triggers go away completely, but most often, the symptoms will diminish greatly over time thereby improving the individual's quality of life.

In most modern Systematic Desensitization programs, the process is broken down into ten steps. This steps are as follows:

1. Initial evaluation. This includes patient history, intake assessment, and explanation of how the therapy works.

2. Relaxation technique training. In this phase, the individual is educated on how to perform tasks such as deep breathing, progressive muscle relaxation, and the visualization of a peaceful place.

3. Overcoming negative self-talk. In this phase, the individual addresses their overestimations of negative outcomes and explores their ability to cope with stressors in order to develop a better understanding. Additionally, individuals will focus on restructuring negative talk into a more constructive thought process.

4. Anxiety coping skills phase. In the step, the individual comes to terms with their symptoms. They address how the symptoms will not completely vanish but that the individual will be better able to cope with symptoms.

5. Imagery desensitization. In this stage, individuals begin to couple coping strategies with stimuli by imagining their triggers and stressors while performing relaxation techniques. Mental exposure is typically done in one minute increments and is progressively increased overtime.

6. Exposure. During this phase, the individual temporarily enters a trigger-related situation in order to practice the breathing and relaxation techniques.

7-9. Exposure Practice phases. In these steps, the individual is exposed to their trigger in several scenarios involving real-life exposure. Initially, they are exposed with a support person, such as therapist, nearby. They will then discuss and address difficulties that may have occurred with the support person. This process is then repeated and continued until the individual is able to manage their triggers without the presence of a support person.

10. Follow-up. In the final step, the therapy is reviewed and summarized for the individual to help in understanding the process. Relapse prevention strategies are developed for the individual to have a plan in the event of a relapse, and the individual discusses closure regarding their treatment.

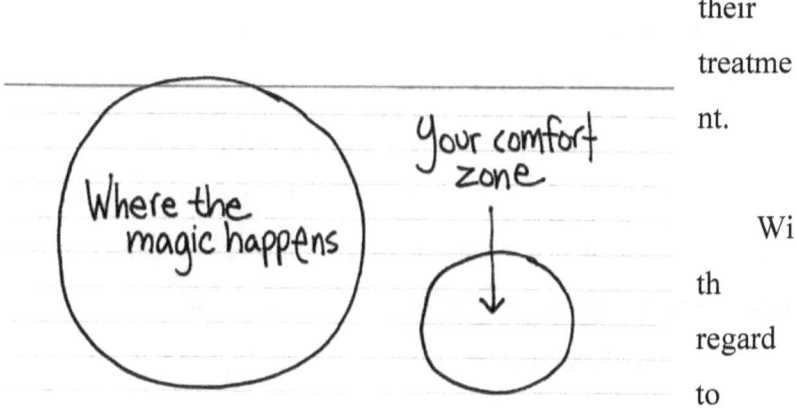

With regard to System Desensitization, there are several issues that many practitioners and therapist have voiced regarding this treatment. The main concern that most people have with this approach to treatment is that it does not address the underlying issues regarding the trauma. The trauma is effective in addressing the behaviors and manifestations of symptoms, but it does ignore the individual's feelings and emotions regarding their triggers. In addition to this, Systematic Desensitization requires individuals to do a large amount of homework outside of the therapy sessions. As many therapists have experienced, clients often fail to do homework because it is time consuming, they lose motivation, or a myriad of other reasons. The homework can often be a significant amount of work in the case of many Systematic Desensitization programs. It is important to continually assess the client's abilities throughout the treatment because pushing a client too hard in this therapy can cause substantial psychological damage and re-traumatization.

During the 1950s and 1960s, several approaches to treatment attempted to address the cognitive piece that was missing from Systematic Desensitization. Two of the most commonly used approaches were Rational Emotive Behavioral Therapy (REBT) and Cognitive Behavioral Therapy (CBT). These two approaches are some of the most commonly used approaches today for treating trauma-related disorders and can be helpful in addressing some of the issues involved with Intergenerational Trauma.

REBT can be easily understood by looking at the ABC model of trauma (activating event, belief, consequence). In addition to the ABC, there is a DEF portion of the model that contains the treatment piece of the model. *D* stands for "disputing or questioning the evidence", *E* stands for "an effective new philosophy", and *F* stands for "new feelings and behaviors." Basically, what occurs in REBT is that a therapist will attempt to change the person's belief associated with their trigger through presenting evidence and disputing the belief. Through a process of utilizing logic and argument, the individual will be able to tear down the dysfunctional belief system and replace it with a new belief system that produces less anxiety and stress.

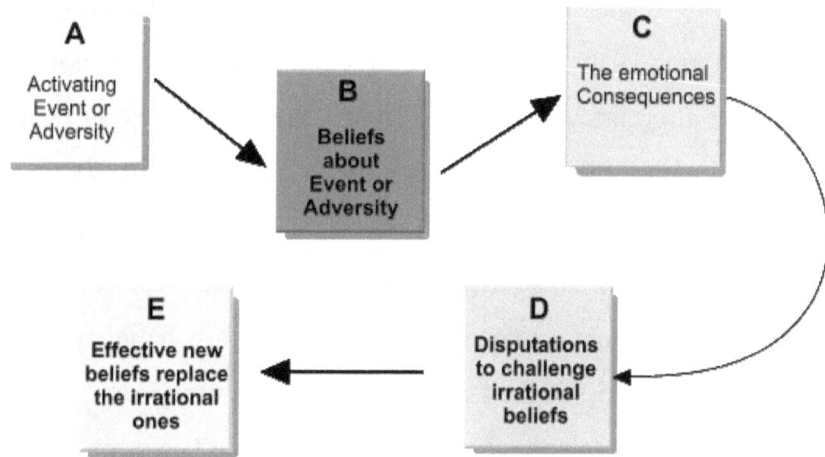

REBT makes several assumptions about the way that human processes and functioning. The approach views thinking, emotion, and action as process that are separate but have significant overlap. Emotion is viewed as a strong and persuasive type of thought process. Behaviors and emotion have impacts on the way in which an individual thinks. In turn, thought and emotion create biases that have an impact and direct the behaviors that an individual performs. As a result of this interplay among the three elements of thought, emotion, and behavior, an individual will develop constructive and helpful belief systems about themselves and their environment, or they will create maladaptive belief systems that cause dysfunction and impairment in their lives.

REBT utilizes the theoretical framework of changing an individual's behaviors that is found in Systematic Desensitization to attempt to change the thinking of an individual about a trigger. When individuals develop a dysfunctional belief system involving triggers, they "catastrophize" the effect of the trigger. In this case, the trigger creates the anxiety-related reaction that releases hormones into their body system and creates the negative experiences associated with PTSD and other disorders. Through REBT, the therapist attempts to re-structure the individual's belief system and re-frame their view of the triggers as items not related to catastrophic consequences. In changing the individual's belief system, their thought process is then changed. The thought process then has an impact on the behaviors that the individual performs and also an impact on the emotions that are experienced in correlation with the trigger.

REBT is one of the most investigated approaches to psychotherapy and has a large body of supporting research to its efficacy. It is, however, not without its limitations and critiques. Many have criticized REBT for being very formula

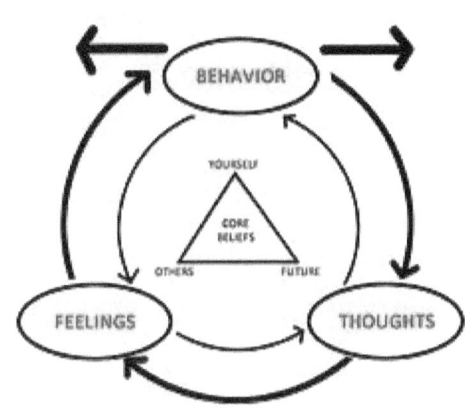

driven in how it is applied. There have many some studies that have produced lackluster results regarding the efficacy of REBT treatments being as low as thirty percent. Even though there have been several critics of the approach, there are still a large number of practitioners who utilize this approach in the treatment of stress-related and trauma-related disorders.

CBT was a psychotherapy that was originally developed to treat depression, but it has since been used to treat a number of disorders and conditions including trauma-related disorders. Throughout the six steps of CBT, individuals will identify critical behaviors relating their disorder, determine if the behaviors are excesses or deficits, determine what their baseline is for the behaviors, and attempt to increase or decrease the targeted behaviors. CBT consists of six phases which include the following: assessment, reconceptualization, skills acquisition, skill consolidation, maintenance, and follow-up. Similar to REBT, CBT was developed through the view that core beliefs are developed through the interaction of thoughts, behaviors, and feelings.

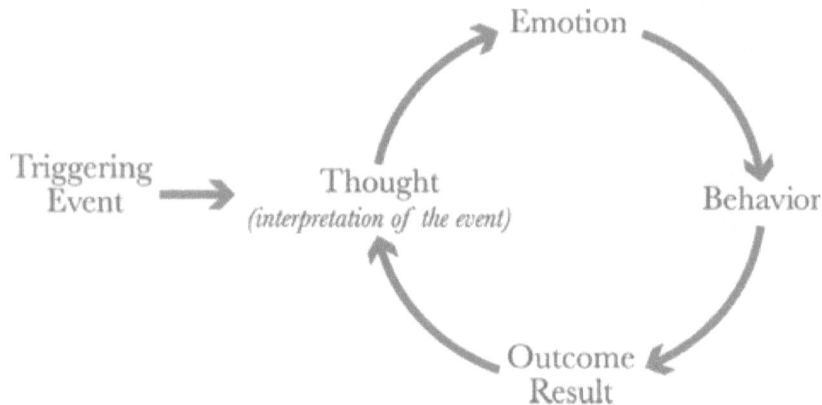

In the early 1980s, a variation of CBT was developed that focused on trauma-related disorders and was especially designed to focus on trauma in children. This variation of CBT is called Trauma Focused Cognitive Behavior Therapy (TF-CBT). Trauma Focused CBT approaches treatment by considering not only the individual's thoughts, behaviors and feelings but also the understanding of the individual's parents and family. This approach served to be one of the first approaches to take into consideration the impact of trauma upon multiple generations. TF-CBT was not designed specifically to focus on the transmission of trauma across generation, but it did address some of the elements that relate to trauma transmission. Throughout therapy, there are some elements that are specific to the child, some that are specific to the parent, and there are some that are jointly applicable to both.

There are eight elements of Trauma Focused CBT. The first element revolved around psychoeducation and parenting skills. This phase focuses on discussion and education about trauma in general and the typical reactions that one can expect as a result of traumatic experience among individuals. During this first phase, the parents receive training on appropriate behavior management techniques and parenting practices that are effective when working with children who have experienced trauma. The second phase involves the development of relaxation techniques. This stages focuses on teaching the child and parents both techniques such as breathing techniques, progressive muscle relaxation, and visual imagery. It is important for the parents to be trained in the relaxation techniques in order to provide support to the child during the implementation of such techniques.

The third phase involves affect expression and regulation. This stage helps the child and parent develop skills and strategies regarding the regulation of emotional reactions that the child may have when presented with reminders of the trauma. In young children, this stage is very important as children have not fully developed the ability to control emotional outbursts. If a parent responds inappropriately to a child's outburst as the result of a trauma trigger, the child may then be further traumatized. In the fourth stage, the therapist helps parents and child understand the cognitive processes that are different in individuals exposed to trauma. During this phase, the family explores the relationships between thoughts, emotions, and actions. In exploring the connections, the family attempts to identify inaccurate connections and provide corrections to the inaccurate concepts that the individuals have developed.

The fifth stage is the trauma narrative and processing stage. This phase begins gradual exposure exercises in which the child will give a narrative of the trauma either verbally, written, or using symbolic representation. During the narrative, the therapist and supporting individuals (i.e. the parents, etc.) will identify concepts and beliefs that may be harmful along with connections that individual has made between the trauma and triggers. In addition to identifying harmful beliefs, the therapist will attempt restructure the individual's harmful beliefs through discussion about the connections the individual may have developed. This process is similar to the disputing phase in REBT treatments. Stage six is the *in vivo* exposure stage. *In vivo* means a live exposure. As the name suggests, the individual is then gradually exposed to live triggers in way that is similar to Systematic Desensitization. This stage aids the individual in learning to control their stress reactions to the triggers in a gradual and safe manner under the supervision of mental health professional.

Stage seven is conjoint stage for parents and children. In this stage, the family works together to enhance their communication about trauma-related issues and create opportunities for healthy discussions about the trauma between the parent and child. It is very important for the family to have a plan in place to be able to discuss the trauma at a later time if needed. Silence often serves to increase the pressure that wells up inside trauma survivors. The final and eight stage of treatment focuses on future growth and further enhancing well-being. The final stage provides the family with information on available resources and provides encouragement for continued maintenance of the skills that were developed throughout therapy.

Trauma-Focused CBT has been proven to be effective in many situations related to trauma. Since the approach is directed towards the treatment of children, the studies have examined its effectiveness in treating the symptoms of PTSD in children. There have over a dozen studies conducted to examine the efficacy of TF-CBT. The studies have found that individuals who have undergone treatment have experienced reductions in anxiety, depression, behavior problems, inappropriate sexualized behavior, and trauma-related shame. Additionally, the studies have found increases in resiliency, trust, interpersonal skills, coping skills, and improved safety skills.

In addition to the therapies that have traditionally been used to treat Post Traumatic Stress Disorder, there have been a few approaches developed in more recent years that focus specifically on Intergenerational Trauma. The intergenerational trauma treatment model (ITTM) was developed as a program that treats not only the trauma that a child may have experienced but also unresolved trauma that a parent may have experienced. This treatment model attempts address the trauma experienced by two different generations simultaneously by focusing on not only the individual's processing of trauma but also the interaction between the parent and child. ITTM incorporates many of the practices of CBT along with activities that focus on the attachment between the parent and the child, parenting skills, affect regulation, and development of competency on the parents' part to handle daily living and life events. The program typically consist of 21 sessions and homework assignments for the parents. The program has been proven to produce results through several clinical reviews conducted.

In addition to therapy, social changes have come about in an attempt to address the causes of large scale historical trauma. These changes have been brought about through legislative changes and changes on societal views of intergenerational trauma. As the issue of intergenerational trauma has gained attention, it has begun to be validated by society as a real issue that has impacted millions of individuals. For the majority of history, such an issue as historical trauma was viewed as being a common thread to many cultures that could simply be forgotten or overlooked, and it would go away and be forgotten. Often it was viewed as "just the way thing are." Even in more recent times, the issue was viewed as being an issue that society could not change because it was in the past. To affect change, one must note that a problem exists and that change can and should occur.

Over the past several decades, there have been a variety of other therapeutic interventions developed and used in the treatment of trauma. The efficacy any practices have not been fully examined in relation to the effects on intergenerational trauma, but as the issue becomes more recognized by society, more studies have begun to focus on intergenerational trauma. Until recently, societal views and focuses have failed to acknowledge and address the impacts of trauma from past generations. The changes in societal views truly be seen as having occurred in the last forty years.

Several policies have been adopted worldwide to address large scale historical traumas. In 1948, the United Nations adopted the Universal Declaration on Human Rights in response to the atrocities that occurred during the Holocaust. Numerous policies regarding human rights that have been enacted have cited the events of the Holocaust. In 1978, the US federal government made changes to its policies regarding the treatment of Native American children by passing the Indian Child Welfare Act (ICWA). ICWA has made attempts to preserve Native American families and culture. This change in policy allowed for state and federal officials to provide services to address the cycles of trauma that had been occurring among Native American families for generations. By enacting legislation and policy to address past traumas of people, many surviving generations are provided with some hope for the prevention of future trauma. This alone does not address the past trauma but does serve as a stepping stone to treatment for many individuals.

As one can note, intergenerational trauma affects hundreds of people and entire cultures. Over the course of history, we hope that humanity learns lessons from past historical events. The occurrences of trauma in the past do not need to be forgotten. The lessons should live on to prevent the reoccurrence of atrocities and the mistreatment of individuals regardless of who they are or from what culture they come. The cultures that we come from should not be forsaken and thrown away through means of assimilation or genocide. Individuals should know who they are and understand their culture and heritage. The deeds and history of ourselves as a human race should have many and produce changes in society as a whole throughout time. Intergenerational trauma has a lot to do with the cultures of people and who they are. We should be able to respect and acknowledge the events, both great and horrific, that our ancestors have gone through, accomplished, and survived. It is important to remember that treating intergenerational trauma is not erasing the culture of an individual or their ties to the past. When viewing the treatment of intergenerational trauma, one should consider the views of the elder generations that had experienced the trauma.

How would generations that experienced trauma in the past and had to live with the PTSD that developed as a result of their traumatic experiences phrase the need for treatment? When working with trauma survivors, I have heard one phrase come up countless times, "I would never want anyone to go through what I went through." No reasonable individual would want their children to experience that kind of trauma. In a similar manner, the treatment of intergenerational trauma is not erasing the culture and heritage of an individual. The culture and heritage should stay intact and be maintained as it provides the individuals with some degree of resiliency. The effects of the trauma is what should be focused on and treated. Improving the quality of life for survivors is the focus of treatment. It is not to erase the past.